PANORAMIC
SOUTH AFRICA

SUNBIRD
PUBLISHING

2 4 6 8 10 9 7 5 3 1

First published 2000

Sunbird Publishing (Pty) Ltd

34 Sunset Avenue, Llandudno, Cape Town, South Africa

Registration number: 4850177827

Copyright © text Sean Fraser

Copyright © photography Alain Proust

Copyright © published edition Sunbird Publishing

Publisher Dick Wilkins

Editor Brenda Brickman

Designer Mandy McKay

Production Manager Andrew de Kock

Reproduction by Unifoto (Pty) Ltd, Cape Town

Printed and bound by Tien Wah Press (Pte) Ltd, Singapore

ISBN 0624037924

Front cover and title page The dolorite formations of
the Karoo's craggy Valley of Desolation have been exposed
by centuries of erosion.

Back cover Wild flowers near Langebaan on the Cape's
West Coast.

Half-title page Tranquil Knysna lagoon lies at the heart
of the southern Cape's most pristine wilderness area.

This page (imprint) The languid Kei River snakes
through this stretch of the Eastern Cape Province, which
was once known as the Transkei, traditional home of the
Xhosa people.

PANORAMIC SOUTH AFRICA

Vast landscapes of rocky scrubland, towering massifs, coastal forest and open veld dotted with spindly acacias; these are but some of the panoramic vistas that stretch across the face of South Africa, a country endowed with an endless string of changing scenes painted by the forces of nature and even, on occasion, the creative hand of its people.

From the very northern reaches of the country – the Northern Province, North-West and Mpumalanga – stretches the splendour of the Lowveld, a wild expanse haunted by the cries of eagles and laced with a series of water courses that cascade across its rolling land, much of which has been battered and sculpted by the unforgiving nature of the elements. The peaks may be dramatic, the valleys sweeping, and the wider region rather dry, but the Lowveld is indeed remarkable in that the rivers and streams that flow here bring to it a life of its own.

Prime among its many gems is that great Eden that is South Africa's most recognised calling card: the famed Kruger National Park, home to an extraordinary array of some the country's most recognisable game species and the holiday/safari destination of hundreds of thousands of visitors every year. Lauded as one of the finest wildlife reserves in the world, Kruger comprises about 20 000 square kilometres of land that varies from bare scrub to undulating grassland, acacia groves and seasonal waters. Boasting nearly 500 bird and 140 mammal species, this rugged land is a paradise of wildlife – from reptiles to

Above The Bourke's Luck Potholes in Mpumalanga were carved by the erosive action of the Blyde and Treur rivers.

amphibians, insects to fish, delicate flowers to lofty baobabs, and the unmistakable awe of its big-game species, among them lion, elephant, buffalo, leopard and rhino, collectively known as the Big Five.

The wide, open spaces and unadulterated views of this African bushveld, the country's most treasured landscape, finally give way to equally impressive scenes provided by the Great Escarpment, closely following the country's perimeter, encircling the highveld plateau with high peaks and steep ravines, sharp ridges and towering mountains.

Standing proud and tall in the heart of the inland plateau enclosed by the Escarpment, is a vibrant and energetic city that saw its humble origins in the embryonic stages of what was to become South Africa's most significant asset and the foundation stone of its

Above The barren landscape of Augrabies is a harsh, near-desert environment.

ever-growing economy. This is Johannesburg, known today as eGoli, or City of Gold, and the centre of the nation's vital mining industry. Although considered by many to be the country's unofficial capital – it is South Africa's biggest and most prominent city, and the most cosmopolitan of all its major centres – it is its sister, Pretoria, to the northeast, that is the country's administrative capital. Long known as the Jacaranda City – for the lilac blossoms that adorn the jacaranda trees during the spring months – Pretoria has, since the earliest days of colonial settlement here, been the centre of the country's political and social development.

Apparently in an entirely different world and yet, in reality, only a few hours' drive from the bustling centres of both Johannesburg and Pretoria, is the fantasy world of the Sun City complex, a grand and imposing vision rising from the dust of the somewhat unforgiving landscape of the Pilanesberg. Reigning supreme over this impressive collection of deluxe hotels is the majestic Palace of the Lost City, wonderland of sweeping staircases, intricate mosaics and crystal chandeliers within marble halls towered over by gilded turrets and swaying palm trees. Set in extensive grounds dotted with man-made lakes, tidal pools and lush forests, the Palace is the heart of Sun City and a magnificent showcase of African hospitality.

In contrast – and, in the northwest, on the opposite side of the country – is the considerably less hospitable Kalahari, an expansive stretch of red earth that extends into both Namibia and Botswana. The searing sands of the Kalahari comprise a semidesert that receives virtually no rain, and yet it has given life to the most enigmatic of southern Africa's people, the ancient San.

In the central part of the country that reaches to the Namibian border is the wonder of the Augrabies Falls National Park, in many parts equally arid, yet most noted for the extraordinary power and spectacle of its tumbling

Above *Much of the outskirts of the Free State town of Harrismith is planted with fields of sunflowers.*

waters, and the setting of the awe-inspiring Augrabies Falls from which it takes its name.

With such splendour covering so much of the countryside, it is easy to forget the parts of the country that are not immediately striking to the eye. Yet, there are vast regions that are not awarded the accolades they so richly deserve.

This is particularly true of the Free State, a gentle but enigmatic region that is, on closer inspection, remarkably attractive in its own way.

The sun-warmed land here is covered either with golden fields of maize or the pastel blooms of wild flowers. But there are wild and rocky expanses too, and the most notable of these is the looming grandeur of the twin buttresses of the Golden Gate, within the confines of the national park of the same name.

Undoubtedly the province's most recognisable landmark, these impressive massifs, however, are destined to compete for status with the immense – and apparently endless – series of peaks and vales that form that great Mountain of the Dragon stretching along the

green-lined coastal belt of the KwaZulu-Natal Midlands, and separating it from the high plateau of the interior.

The ridged peaks of the Drakensberg, the spine of the Great Escarpment, has been carved by millennia of erosion, lending to this most revered of southern Africa's ranges a sense of awe unsurpassed by any of the other vast inland mountains. The Drakensberg, much of which is painted with vibrant shades of emerald in spring, gentle yellows in summer, earth tones in autumn, and blanketed in white in winter, is one magnificent and breathtaking peak and sweeping valley after the next.

At the foot of the northern stretch of these great slopes, skirting the coastal environment of forests, lakes, rivers and streams, are the placid waters of the Greater St Lucia Wetland Park, a reserve established to protect the sensitive balance of nature that covers so much of this shoreline. The waters of the lake – and, indeed, the Indian Ocean – harbour an extraordinary array of flora and fauna endemic to a region that extends from Kosi Bay in the north, through the Maputaland Marine Reserve to Sodwana and beyond.

Above The 40 000-hectare Mkuze Game Reserve lies to the northwest of the St Lucia wetlands.

But the magnificent natural heritage of KwaZulu-Natal does not end at the beachfront or the shores of its great lake. The rolling hills and undulating countryside also form the backdrop to some of its most prominent – and applauded – wildlife reserves, which continue to emphasise the importance of conserving the rich heritage of the region. This is especially true when one considers the exceptional efforts of the rangers and conservationists of parks such as Hluhluwe-Umfolozi, which have contributed in no small way to the re-establishment of the white rhino in the area.

On the other hand, the metropolitan centre that forms the nucleus of wild and beautiful KwaZulu-Natal is the city of Durban, a thriving metropolis with a past steeped in a rich and varied history that stems from the cultures of the many peoples who call this province home. Emerging from a past that earned it the name of the Last Colonial Outpost, Durban is today one of the country's most diverse and exciting centres, a magical mix of the cosmopolitan and the rural, boasting a vital bay and an expansive coastline that has made it one of South Africa's most popular holiday and tourist destinations.

Worlds away from the bright lights of the big city is KwaZulu-Natal's Valley of a Thousand Hills, a wide expanse of indigenous fauna sprawled across the tropical countryside of the province's east coast. It is also along this rugged and, in places, savage coast – albeit further

south – that we encounter the aptly named Wild Coast. Although the hinterland comprises a patchwork of cultivated farmland, the coast itself is, despite its magnificent panorama of endless beach and dune-lined shore, somewhat volatile, lashed every so often by the most tumultuous of seas. Holding court over the many delightful bays and hamlets that nestle along the shore – St Fancis Bay, Jeffrey's Bay and Kenton-on-Sea are but a few – is another old colonial settlement that has remained true to its cultural heritage, and yet moved with aplomb into the twenty-first century: Port Elizabeth is the city that now stands on the site where the first European settlers first stepped ashore on the beaches of what is today known as the Eastern Cape Province.

It is this sometimes wild, sometimes welcoming land that stretches into the most scenic of South Africa's coastal strips, forming the awe-inspiring beauty of the Cape's Garden Route. Of all the wondrous spots that lay sprinkled along the natural splendour of this shore – many of which are prime holiday destinations for both

Above The wilderness around Knysna is a land of lakes and lagoons.

locals and visitors – Plettenberg Bay remains the most fashionable of getaways. The town, a relatively untamed haven for outdoor activities – not least of which is its pristine shoreline – caters largely for the holidaymakers that make their way there on the annual pilgrimage in search of sun, surf and sand. Considerably more subdued and, to some degree, catering for the less adventurous vacationer, is the charming little town of Knysna, virtually surrounded by the forest glades for which it has become famous. This is the home of the vibrantly feathered Knysna lourie and the pansy shells that litter its beaches. Knysna originated in the early days of forestry on the east coast, and is today a welcoming host to holidaymakers who come not only for the solitude and to admire the tall yellowwoods and stinkwoods that make up its famed forests, but to explore the lagoon – dominated by the imposing Knysna Heads, and the nearby National Lake Area, much of which comprises conserved areas.

The changing panorama of this countryside is most noticeable as the gentle coastal towns give way to the rugged, rocky scenery of the Karoo that extends into the interior to form the Little Karoo – the setting for small but thriving towns such as Oudtshoorn – and the Great Karoo, a sometimes forlorn and windswept semidesert with a beauty of its own.

Further west, just inland from the Cape's West Coast – a rugged shore rich in flora and fauna both on the land and in its life-giving waters, and thriving fishing centre – is the wonderland of Namaqualand. For at least 10 months of the year this expanse, apparently barren and lifeless, suddenly bursts into bloom after the spring rains, sprinkling the veld with vast patches of yellow, purple, red and green as the wild flowers come to life for the annual spectacle that continues to attract thousands of amazed visitors year after year. The surrounding lands then seem to take on a very different panorama, one dotted with antelope and mountain zebra quite at home among the

Above *The historic town of Stellenbosch is the heart of wine country.*

flowers that cover the Strandveld, Hantam, the Knersvlakte, Bokkeveld, and the majestic Cederberg, sculpted by centuries of eroding elements and home of the Clanwilliam cedar *(Widdringtonia cedarbergensis)*.

In stark contrast to the rocky landscape is the flourishing Hex River Valley and the mountains that skirt its orchards and vineyards. These fertile soils yield some of the world's finest fruits, which are matched only by the exceptional grapes of the farmlands around Franschhoek and Stellenbosch, the centre of the country's wine industry and the heart of the world-renowned Wine Route that winds through the gentle lands on the outskirts of the Mother City.

The Cape Peninsula is today South Africa's premier tourist destination, a unique blend of cosmopolitan life with an extraordinarily rich history and an exceptional natural heritage that stretches from coast to coast. The city of Cape Town comprises an amalgamation of a vibrant City Bowl and the many 'villages' that spread along its coast from the beaches of the Atlantic suburbs down the ridge of mountains that form its spine, past

Muizenberg to the naval post of Simon's Town and beyond to the pristine wilderness of Cape Point. This most southerly finger of the peninsula lies within the Cape of Good Hope Nature Reserve, itself part of the new Cape Peninsula National Park that starts at the heart of Cape Town on the slopes of its magical Table Mountain, also home to that botanic wonder known simply as Kirstenbosch to the more than two million visitors who make their way here every year.

The great mountain, bedecked with hectares of fynbos and other indigenous vegetation, in turn, looks over the waters of Table Bay and beyond to the tiny World Heritage Site known to the world as Robben Island, once a leper colony and the prison that held former State President Nelson Mandela, and today a living museum dedicated to those who fought for the democratisation of South Africa and its people.

These are the many faces and panoramas of a country blessed with the wonder of wide, open spaces, the gentle power of a winding coastline and the rocky outcrops of its protective mountains. This is panoramic South Africa.

Left and opposite Although much of the Mpumalanga environment is often associated with parched and somewhat inhospitable conditions during the region's dry winter months, the undulating landscape may in certain areas, particularly in the rainy summer months, be both lush and productive.

Overleaf Named after a local gold prospector, Thomas Bourke, the unusual sculptures that comprise the Bourke's Luck potholes were created over thousands of years by the weathering action of the waters of the Blyde River.

Previous pages Extraordinary rock formations, carved over millennia by the erosive action of wind and water, frame God's Window and stand sentinel over the untamed wilderness the of Mpumalanga landscape.

Right The 90-metre Lisbon Falls is but one of a number of impressive of waterfalls that cascade through Mpumalanga's often dry and rugged panorama, where many of the water courses carried a wealth of alluvial gold.

Left Ribbons of water tumble down the rocky faces of the Mpumalanga landscape, gathering in lush groves at the foot of sparkling waterfalls.

Above From the craggy ramparts of God's Window, the dense thickets of the Mpumalanga veld stretch toward the distant horizon.

Opposite Although in parts rather dry, the Mpumalanga wilderness is laced with an extensive network of water courses, many of which originate in these hills and valleys.

Above and opposite The jagged ridges of the Mpumalanga Escarpment give way to dramatic rock formations characteristic of the Lowveld, a region pitted with breathtaking canyons and valleys, most of which are blessed with rivers, streams and waterfalls that enhance its stark beauty.

Overleaf The dry winter of the Northern Province's Kruger National Park, the most renowned of the country's abundant wildlife and nature reserves and wildly popular with both local and foreign holidaymakers, is the best time to view the area's plentiful game, that gather at the few remaining water holes to slake their thirst.

Above In the dry winter months experienced in the Lowveld, the grasses of the game-rich Kruger Park turn russet, often hiding a pride of lion whose natural coloration blends well with the surrounding veld.

Opposite In contrast to the aridity of the winter veld, the rains of the summer months bring welcome respite to the Kruger National Park, and the banks of the Olifants River erupt in a blaze of green.

Previous pages The northern stretch of the Great Escarpment – the grand string of mountains and hills that separates the vast internal plateau of the subcontinent from its coastal fringe – is dotted with aloes, typical vegetation of the land that extends westwards into the interior.

Above The imposing Union Buildings in Pretoria, Gauteng, designed by one of the country's most prolific and revered architects Sir Herbert Baker, was finally finished in 1913, and is for at least six months of year – when parliament is not based in Cape Town – the seat of national government.

Above The country's administrative capital, Pretoria, long a centre of political activity and still a seat of government – an honour it shares with Cape Town – is often considered one of South Africa's most picturesque cities, most recognisable by the rows of lilac-bloomed jacaranda trees that line its pretty streets.

Overleaf left Set along the slopes of a hilltop above Johannesburg, the grand Westcliff Hotel looks out over the modern city that sprawls out in all directions at its feet.
Overleaf right The city of Johannesburg rose from the dusty veld as a small, makeshift shanty town in the early days of the country's gold rush to become eGoli, the Place of Gold.

Previous pages With its gilded turrets, embellished stonework and romantic associations with Darkest Africa, the Palace of the Lost City at Sun City in the North-West Province is undoubtedly the grandest and most impressive resort complex on the continent.

Left Despite the fact that the Sun City complex is entirely landlocked by the often dry and rugged terrain of the hinterland and far from the roar of the ocean, holidaymakers have at their disposal an impressive stretch of beach specially constructed for their pleasure.

Opposite Sited as one of South Africa's most popular tourist drawcards, the exceptional array of attractions to the Palace of the Lost City includes the extraordinary Valley of the Waves, a marine adventure in the heart of the bushveld.

Previous pages The arid and apparently inhospitable Kalahari Gemsbok National Park
in the Northern Cape is the heart of the traditional homeland of the ancient San people,
and recently merged with Botswana's Gemsbok National Park to form the expansive
Kgalagadi Transfrontier Park, the first of its kind to be established as a multi-national effort
to conserve wildest Africa.

Left The powerful surge of the great Orange River gushes through the granite gorge that
winds its way through the stark wilderness of Augrabies Falls National Park.

Above Despite its Korana name, meaning 'great waters', the Augrabies Falls National Park
is often rather dry, stretching across endless plains apparently devoid of life but, in fact, home
to a number of wildlife species.

Opposite The expansive landscape of Augrabies Falls National Park was first proclaimed
a conservation area more than 30 years ago, but was only recently expanded to incorporate
the region of Riemvasmaak and now totals in excess of 80 000 hectares of protected land.

Overleaf The granite chasm that guides the torrential waters of the Orange through
the Augrabies region when the river is at its peak in the summer months extends some
18 kilometres and is more than 200 metres deep in places along its sometimes violent course.

Above Solitude and a sense of abandonment appears
to pervade much of the Northern Cape. The vegetation
around Steinkopf – inland from Port Nolloth and north
of Springbok – is quite unique to this part of the world
and lends to it a life of its own.

Right Amid a land that can prove to be very harsh indeed,
with extremes of climate and temperature, is the tranquil
and lush Eye of Kuruman, the source of the river that feeds
the small Northern Cape town and nourishes its lands.

Overleaf Painted with the golden hues of its sparse
vegetation and draped in the wide blue yonder of its sky
is the small hamlet of Aggeneys, seemingly lost in the
expanse of the endless landscape of the dry Northern Cape.

Previous pages Although remarkable in themselves, the sandstone buttresses that dominate the Golden Gate Highlands National Park in the Free State are further enhanced and illuminated by the last light of day.

Left Although winter brings a blanket of snow to the loftiest peaks of the great Drakensberg, the summer sees hills of this mighty range bedecked with a mantle of green, as the rolling hills emerge after an icy winter.

Above Protruding from among the high peaks of KwaZulu-Natal's Drakensberg is the distinctive facade of Giant's Castle, one of the great pinnacles that form the 'barrier of spears', the description bestowed upon it by the Zulus.

Opposite The face of the Drakensberg range alters dramatically with the change of seasons. The winter mantle of the Drakensberg is a blanket of white snow that covers the highest peaks of a range that extends along much of the eastern front of the Great Escarpment.

Overleaf The verdant slopes of the Drakensberg are home to one of the region's most notable game reserves – that at Giant's Castle, nestled between the lofty summit of Cathedral Peak and the precarious Sani Pass, and noted for the conservation efforts surrounding eland and raptors.

Left Blessed with such an abundance of untamed wilderness and an extraordinarily rich natural heritage, a significant proportion of KwaZulu-Natal has been given over to game reserves. Prime among these is the more than 30 000 hectares of Itala Game Reserve, stretching along the course of the Pongolo River.

Opposite The life-giving Pongola River — watering ground for an assortment of big game — pumps through a valley of the same name to form the natural border between KwaZulu-Natal and the kingdom of Swaziland.

Overleaf The 38 000 hectares of savanna that covers the Mkuzi Game Reserve is a haven for a variety of wildlife, but most particularly the waterbirds that flock here to nest and make their home along the waters of both the Mkuze River and the Nsumu Pan.

Previous pages The often turbulent waters of the Umgeni River tumble some 95 metres into a deep gorge to form KwaZulu-Natal's spectacular Howick Falls. Situated as it is above the falls, an old path worn by early European settlers offers visitors a number of impressive viewing sites.

Right KwaZulu-Natal is the traditional home of the Nguni-speaking Zulu nation, which has inhabited the region for centuries. As a result, many areas – such as the Zulu village near Eshowe – are still home to small tribal communities that remain true to the customs of their ancestors.

Previous pages Traditional fish kraals of Tonga locals stud the gentle waters of Maputaland's Kosi Bay, a vital link in the marine ecosystem that today forms part of the extensive Greater St Lucia Wetland Park to the south.

Left Long considered the seat of government for colonial powers in KwaZulu-Natal, the modern city of Durban still echoes its European heritage, but also incorporates into the cityscape the influences of tropical Africa and its subtropical vegetation.

Above Durban is South Africa's third largest metropolitan centre, integrating its vital economic contribution to the national economy with the abundant beachfront facilities that continue to attract an ever-growing tourist market.

Opposite Often temperamental, yet always breathtaking in its spectacle, the eastern shoreline that stretches past Durban is punctuated by high-rise buildings typical of a first world city.

Overleaf left Tucked away in the tranquil landscape that skirts the KwaZulu-Natal coast near Ballito is Zimbali Lodge, a fine example of an ever-growing hospitality industry that takes full advantage of the attractions of the southern African wilderness.

Overleaf right The ruggedly beautiful coastal strip just north of Durban provides the remarkable background to Umhlanga Rocks, a beachfront haven for the holidaymakers who make their annual migration to the shores of the warm Indian Ocean.

Below The Eastern Cape's Wild Coast comprises an endless stretch of beach that borders a sometimes savage ocean, which in turn dictates much of the human activity along this pristine expanse, dominated here by Cob Inn. **Opposite** The mouth of the small Kwanyane River, having wound its way across the scenic hinterland and down the coastal plain, opens into the great Indian Ocean. **Overleaf** This stretch of the Eastern Cape, through which snakes the languid Kei River, was once known as the Transkei, the traditional home of the Xhosa people.

Previous pages The course of the Umgeni River winds its way through the dales that skirt the seemingly endless number of knolls that dot the undulating countryside of KwaZulu-Natal's aptly named Valley of a Thousand Hills.
Above Not for nothing is much of the Eastern Cape shoreline known as the 'wild coast', buffeted as it is by an all-too-often ruthless Indian Ocean, bringing to grief many an ill-prepared vessel along its rocky beach, including the *Jacaranda*, in 1971.

Previous pages The citizens of, and visitors to, Port Elizabeth, varyingly described as the Friendly City and the Windy City, celebrate the harbour town's most distinctive characteristics at the yacht basin, hub of weekend leisure activities in the Eastern Cape.

Above Typical of the small hamlets that mark the plentiful bays and coves that line the east coast of the southern Cape is the village of Cape St Francis, situated on the peninsula-like headland that guards the entrance to St Francis Bay.

Right Cape St Francis, but one of the many jewels that stud the remarkable shoreline of the Cape's Garden Route, is in the winter months often buffeted by the northwesterly winds that conjure up the swells and waves that make this coastal town a Mecca for dare-devil surfers from all over the world.

Left The curve of beach that shadows the Robberg Peninsula also marks the border of the Robberg Nature Reserve, playground for the seals that visit its sands, the dolphins that ply its waters and the Cape cormorants that wing across its sky.

Bottom left Most often lauded as the Jewel of South Africa's Garden Route, Plettenberg Bay – with its endless beaches, spectacular sunrises, and landmark Beacon Isle Hotel – attracts more than 100 000 visitors during the peak holiday season.

Below Much of the scenic Garden Route comprises stretches of sensitive ecosystems officially protected in order to conserve its sealife, including the bottlenose dolphins that play offshore.

Opposite Acclaimed as one of the most panoramic coastal strips in the world, popular Lookout Beach on Plettenberg Bay is but one of the many unspoiled spots that form the chain of picturesque vistas that is the scenic Garden Route.

Above Chugging its way over the bridge that crosses the Knysna Lagoon is the ever-popular Outeniqua Choo-Tjoe, a narrow-gauge steam locomotive that ferries visitors through the lushly wooded wilderness of the Outeniqua landscape.

Right Knysna Lagoon, a magnificent marine wilderness in its own right, is flanked by the sandstone monoliths of what are commonly referred to as The Heads. These towering headlands provide not only remarkable views over the water and the famed resort town, but the western head also incorporates the protected wilderness of the Featherbed Nature Reserve.

Above The scenic route that follows the southeastern coastline of the country is studded with small hamlets, many of which were established early in the 19th century.
Opposite The tiny village of Great Brak River, some 26 kilometres from Mossel Bay, lies along the banks of the river of the same name that flows into the sea here.

Overleaf Tucked away in the rugged highlands of the Eastern Cape is the Mountain Zebra National Park, home of one of the world's rarest mammals and the setting for an extraordinary conservation effort that ensured that numbers of this zebra have grown from about 10 to over 200 individuals since the proclamation of the park in the late 1930s.

Left Established at the height of the Victorian era, the little town of Matjiesfontein, meaning 'mat fountain' – named for the abundance of local reeds used to weave mats – remains true to the character of its past, with the grand old Lord Milner Hotel taking pride of place in the centre of the town.

Opposite Bordered by a narrow range of hills on an otherwise flat landscape, the wide, open spaces that still envelop the Northern Cape district around Matjiesfontein are sparsely vegetated and suffer extremes of temperature, bitterly cold in winter and blazingly hot during the searing summer months.

Right Scattered across the expanse of the Great Karoo is a series of small hamlets, many of which – despite their Dutch names – have distinctly English colonial origins and are typically Victorian in style if not in character. One such place is the charming village of Prince Albert, which still boasts the fine architecture of yesteryear.

Previous pages Standing proud, tall and handsomely rugged in the southern region of the Great Karoo are the towering cliffs the Valley of Desolation, a series of sheer dolerite columns that protrude from the craggy landscape to watch over the small Karoo towns.

Above and opposite The Valley of Desolation once formed the outer limits of the frontier in colonial days, and the nearby town of Graaff-Reinet remains a thriving little centre with a rich but turbulent past.

Previous pages and above Although for most of the year the Namaqualand region in the northern reaches of the Western Cape may appear unforgivingly harsh and inhospitable, punctuated only occasionally by the stark limbs of a simple kokerboom, the gentle spring rains bring with them a profusion of floral colour.

Opposite Much of the interior of the Cape West Coast interior is a virtual desert for up to 10 months of a year that sees only a meagre rainfall and appears to harbour only the succulents that thrive here, but the apparently unavailing landscape springs to life for a brief few weeks in August and September.

Left The West Coast, rugged in its beauty but blessed with an abundant sealife, has long been a vital fishing haven, and the folk of small towns, such as Paternoster, have for centuries depended on the sea harvest for their livelihood.

Above Not as well-known as the expansive West Coast National Park of which it forms part, the Postberg Nature Reserve is nevertheless graced with an equally remarkable seascape, offset in spring by an impressive floral display.

Opposite The fishing village of Paternoster lies tucked away on the rocky stretch of the Cape West coast, and its tranquil environs and unspoilt landscape are becoming a popular getaway for city folk.

Overleaf Wild flowers will always be synonymous with out-of-the-way spots such Lookout Point in Langebaan on the Cape West coast, and the annual eruption of colour on an otherwise somewhat desolate landscape remains its most important tourism drawcard.

Above The rocky outcrops of the Pakhuis Pass near Clanwilliam is typical of the broken and craggy countryside of the West Coast interior, strewn with boulders, and yet well within the boundaries of the floral wonderland that emerges in early spring.

Opposite Stark and seemingly uninviting, the boulder-strewn Cederberg region – dominated by the 2 000-metre-high Sneeuberg – is named for the rare Clanwilliam cedar once common on the stony mountainside, but now protected within the confines of a reserve, nevertheless spectacular in it beauty.

Overleaf As the winter snows that cap the sandstone peaks of the Hex River mountain range near Ceres begin to melt, the resulting streams lace through the valley, feeding both the untamed wilderness and the cultivated lands below.

Opposite Widely acclaimed as one of South Africa's premium wine-producing regions, the Franschhoek Valley in the Western Cape was first settled by Europeans in the 17th century, and it was these the pioneers in viticulture who planted the vineyards that today produce some of the country's finest wines.

Overleaf Simonsberg, named after the Dutch governor Simon van der Stel, forms the spectacular backdrop to the historic town of Stellenbosch – also named in memory of the governor – which is today the heartland of the country's wine industry and a popular attraction for visitors travelling into the Cape interior.

Previous pages The Hex River valley, embraced by the craggy arm of mountains of the same name that tower over it, is both rich and fertile, blessed not only with the seasonal streams that run down the slopes to nurture the vegetation but also an above-average rainfall.

Above The orchards and vineyards that stretch across the land nestled in the shadow of the snow-capped Kouebokkeveld mountains produce not only some of the finest export-quality fruit, but have also become world-famous for the region's exceptional fortified wines.

Right On the perimeter of the Little Karoo lie scattered a number of small towns, such as Montagu, which have made an enormous success of the orchards that thrive in the fertile valleys of the generally rugged Koo region.

Above Straddling the foothills of the steep and, in places, impassable Riviersonderend mountains, is the tiny village of McGregor whose townsfolk, relatively isolated from frenetic city life, continue to live a somewhat simple existence in this remote district.

Opposite The road through Calvinia in the Northern Cape winds through the small Karoo town, crosses the mountainous stretch that separates the Roggeveldberge in the south and the smaller Hantamsberge in the north, and then stretches beyond into the vastness of the Great Karoo.

Overleaf The little fishing hamlet of Arniston – also known over time as Waenhuiskrans – remains one of those quiet, laid-back towns on the southern Cape coast where the simple life is interrupted infrequently by the occasional visitor in search of solitude.

Above Like many of the little inlets that line much of the Cape Peninsula, the cove at St James – with its gentle tidal pool and row of brightly coloured bathing boxes – saw its heyday in the early years of the 19th century, when holidaymakers from all over the country sought solace in the fresh sea air that wafts off False Bay.

Opposite Muizenberg, scene of the famous battle for supremacy over the Cape that was fought on the mountain slopes above the sleepy suburb, is today a haven for the bonhomie of surfers and sunworshippers who flock to the white sands that start below Boyes Drive and stretch to Sunrise Beach and beyond.

Previous pages South African naval and maritime history starts and ends in Simon's Bay, the small but busy inlet that forms the heart of Simonstown and gateway to the southern peninsula.

Right A breeding colony of jackass penguins – named after the bray-like call of mature adults – has established itself at the protected enclave of Boulders on the False Bay coast. This close-knit group is considerably smaller than the 100 000-strong colony that has found a home on Dassen Island off the western coast of South Africa.

Below The natural heritage of the Cape Peninsula is at its most bountiful on the mountainous coastal strip that stretches along the shores of False Bay to Cape Point. It is here, at Boulders Beach, that one of the Cape's protected bird species, the jackass penguin, has established a home.

Left Layers of sandstone form the massive more than 1 000-metre bulk of Table Mountain, and it is on these hardy slopes that are found an extraordinary array of plant species (nearly as many as are found in the entire United Kingdom) and a variety of wildlife, from rock hyraxes (or dassies), to porcupines and Himalayan tahrs – which conservationists plan to remove and replace with indigenous species.

Opposite The smart new restaurant facilities at the summit of the mountain provide welcome amenities for the many visitors who walk up the slopes, or glide up in the cable cars to see the Mother City from its most famous viewing site.

Overleaf On the western flank of Table Mountain stands the looming hulk of Lion's Head, the nearly 700 metres of which provide popular walking trails – in places, quite demanding, and especially risky when mists roll in from the ocean.

Previous pages Castle Rock is perhaps one of the most recognisable beacons that mark the Kirstenbosch National Botanic Gardens, the world-famous botanical wonderland visited by hundreds of thousands of both locals and foreigners annually for its extensive range of indigenous vegetation, including thousands of species of Cape fynbos.

Right Cape Town's most famous landmark – and, along with Kirstenbosch and the Victoria & Alfred Waterfront, the Mother City's most popular tourist attraction – is the flat-topped monolith of Table Mountain, where new, modern cable cars carry armies of excited visitors to the top – and down again – to catch a bird's-eye view of Table Bay and beyond.

Above Today a Natural Heritage Site and living museum dedicated to those who served prison sentences here during the struggle for democracy in South Africa, Robben Island lies nearly 12 kilometres from Table Bay and the Mother City that lines its shores.

Opposite Now that the island has moved beyond its tainted past as a leper colony and penitentiary, Robben Island, with its rock-strewn yet inviolate landscape, is a favourite attraction for sightseers, who are shuttled to the island from that other city drawcard, the V&A Waterfront, on the Makana ferry.

Overleaf As witnessed by thousands of postcards and in many a collection of holiday photographs, Table Bay – as seen from the sandy white beaches of Blouberg on the other side of the bay – lies at the foot of Table Mountain, Cape Town's most famous landmark.

Previous pages Since the establishment of the early replenishment station by Dutch colonialists in the 17th century, Table Bay has remained a vital link between southern Africa and the rest of the world. Today, much of the dockland is devoted to the city's busy harbour, but the V&A Waterfront leisure and entertainment complex centred around the Victoria Basin has once again drawn Cape Town's people to the water's edge.

Left Because Cape Town is so ideally located on a remarkably pristine peninsula, Capetonians and visitors to the Mother City spend much of their leisure time on the beach, making the Sea Point waterfront – with its promenade stretching along its length, and an endless thread of restaurants and night spots – a popular choice for fun-seekers.

Above At its most fashionable in the late 1930s and early '40s, when much of the elite of Cape society kept homes along this seafront, the Atlantic suburb of Sea Point remains a hub of activity: busy shopping malls and specialist businesses do a sound trade by day and, by night, clubs and restaurants burst at the seams with lively patrons.

Opposite On the outskirts of the City Bowl, right at the water's edge, lies Green Point, tucked between the burgeoning V&A Waterfront on the city's foreshore and Sea Point. It is here, in the suburb's sports stadium, that Cape minstrels serenade and entertain the public during the annual New Year festivities.

Opposite The seascape of Clifton comprises a row of four equally impressive beaches, separated from each other by conglomerations of boulders. Each sunny spot tends to cater for a particular crowd, from active young sun-seekers to family groups.

Overleaf Cradled as it is in the gentle curve of shore that winds its way along the Atlantic seaboard, the slope above Clifton, with Lion's Head guarding it and vistas that extend way into the distant horizon, is prime real estate in Cape Town, and is studded with one inspiring home after another.

Above and right The most notable characteristic of the splendid Atlantic suburbs is the string of wondrous beaches that line this shore. Protected from the winds that often plague other sandy stretches along the peninsula, the pristine sands of Bakoven, Bantry Bay, Camps Bay, Clifton (pictured here) and Llandudno are the most popular among beachgoers.

Above In the distant foothills of the gnarled finger of the peninsula mountain range lie the tranquil and secluded beaches of Llandudno and Sandy Bay.

Opposite From a rocky vantage point of Maiden's Cove on the heel of the foot that is the Cape Peninsula, the Twelve Apostles range – comprising 17 rather than just 12 rugged peaks in succession – extends south towards Hout Bay.

Overleaf A panorama seldom recorded or recognised even by Capetonians is the rear edifice, from the vantage point of Duikerpoint in Hout Bay, of the famed Table Mountain, from which extends for several kilometres the rugged peaks of the Twelve Apostles. It is this stretch of rocky ridges that forms the spine of the Cape Peninsula National Park, headed by the slopes of Table Mountain. In the foreground are the beaches of Llandudno and Sandy Bay.

Opposite The lofty crest of Chapman's Peak – at no less than 600 metres above sea level – provides the ideal lookout point from which to view the expansive panorama of Hout Bay, and the long, snaking shoreline that encircles the sheltered little bay below.

Overleaf Winding Chapman's Peak Drive, cut by the hand of mankind through the steep gradient of the mountain slopes, sweeps for some 10 kilometres from Hout Bay through to Noordhoek on its southern side. Unseasonal rains have been known to dislodge precariously situated boulders on the mountainside, and to avoid mishaps, this most scenic of Cape Town's drives may on occasion be closed to traffic.

Previous pages One of the Cape's most fiercely protected natural havens is the centuries-old fishing town of Hout Bay. Although the village once depended almost entirely on the timber yielded by its thickly wooded mountain slopes, it is its old fishing harbour that remains the lifeline of many of the fisherfolk who still inhabit the upper reaches of the valley.

Above and right The prominent landmark, The Sentinel, watches over the citizens of Hout Bay, who – tucked away in this semi-rural haven of tranquility – take enormous pride in the splendid natural heritage of what they like to think of as the 'Republic of Hout Bay'.

Above and opposite The serene little village of Noordhoek may be the domain of laid-back artists and poets, but the long expanse of its pristine white sands is there for all to enjoy. On lazy Sunday afternoons locals walk their dogs or ride their horses along the beach or simply take a stroll to catch their breath, while summer holidays bring the visitors who have 'discovered' this paradise.

Overleaf Although the entire peninsula has been incorporated into the all-encompassing Cape Peninsula National Park, the jewel in this enviable crown is the virginal wilderness of the Cape of Good Hope Nature Reserve at the southern tip. It is here that the headland of Cape Point, for centuries its rocky shore the bane of passing maritime traffic, is whipped by the waves of the unrelenting Atlantic.